Flow[illegible]o Fred does it again!

Eira Reeves

On Tuesday, Duncan decided to deliver some potted plants to the flower shop customers. Flora helped to put them on the delivery cycle. Fred just watched.

Then, Flora lifted Fred into the basket at the back of the cycle, so that he could go for a ride too!

Duncan waved goodbye to Flora and said he would see her later. Fred settled down to enjoy his ride.

On the way, people stopped and pointed at Fred.
They had never seen a dog riding a bike before!

Duncan stopped outside Miss Bright's house. He took one potted plant from the front basket, and told Fred to sit still while he delivered it.

One minute went by and Fred sat still . . . until he saw a cat move behind the fence. Now, **she** would be fun to play with!

Fred couldn't wait any longer. Suddenly, he leapt from the basket and began to chase her.

Fred chased the cat round and round and round. They circled Duncan and Miss Bright until they all felt very giddy.

The animals leapt and jumped across the lawn. Fred really enjoyed the chase – even when a rake fell over and nearly hit him on the nose.

The cat climbed up a tree. Fred tried to follow, but he got stuck for a while on a branch!

Finally the cat jumped into a birdbath and began to busy herself washing. Fred tried to reach her, but couldn't. The garden looked a terrible mess.

Poor Fred! He got such a telling off from Duncan. The cat just smiled and pretended that the terrible mess had nothing to do with her!

Meanwhile, Duncan had a great idea. He took all the potted plants from his cycle and planted them in Miss Bright's garden.

Miss Bright was delighted. Her garden had never looked so beautiful. Her neighbours thought the garden looked so lovely, they ordered lots of plants from Duncan.

Duncan was so pleased with all the orders, he stopped at the butchers on the way home to buy Fred a big bone. Fred was pleased too!